SECRETS
TO A KICKASS
MARRIAGE

Marriage Guide to Living
Your Dream Life

SECRETS
TO A KICKASS
MARRIAGE

Marriage Guide to Living
Your Dream Life

MIDORI A. VERITY

Disclaimer

The purpose of this book is to educate and entertain. The author or publisher does not guarantee that anyone following the techniques, suggestions, tips, ideas, or strategies will become successful. The author and publisher shall have neither liability or responsibility to anyone with respect to any loss or damage caused, or alleged to be caused, directly or indirectly, by the information contained in this book.

Printed in the United States of America.

TABLE OF CONTENTS

Dedications vii

Introduction to Having a Kickass Marriage 1

Chapter 1: Dream Together. Dream Big! 5

Chapter 2: It's All in the Attitude 13

Chapter 3: Achieving Your Ultimate Life 23

Chapter 4: Who is that in Your Bed? 29

Chapter 5: Live Sexy—Get Your Mojo Back! 37

Chapter 6: Communication That Works! 51

Chapter 7: Cheat Sheet To the Opposite Sex 59

Chapter 8: Reigniting the Passion 63

Chapter 9: Financial Freedom 81

Chapter 10: Maintaining Your New Lifestyle 87

About Midori Verity—It Started with a Midlife Crisis! 91

DEDICATIONS

For Bill, my fabulous, supportive, and insanely patient husband. You encourage me to fly!

For Nicholas and Chandler, my kids who inspire me to be my best.

For Kate, for living fearlessly, demonstrating the importance of focusing on what truly matters, and forgetting the rest of the b.s.

INTRODUCTION TO HAVING A KICKASS MARRIAGE

Today's modern relationship involves insane burdens! To maintain a long-term, healthy marriage you're expected to practice romance, maintain an exciting sexual lifestyle, and be emotionally supportive. You are also striving for financial abundance, an equal share in household chores, and trying to raise your children to be super star prodigies of the world. Of course, you need to do all this while also looking and feeling fantastic!

My first bit of advice, STOP TRYING SO HARD!

How close are you to this idealistic couple? If you aren't quite there, no worries. Who expects all this from you? Chances are, it's the person looking back at you in the mirror. **There is no such thing as a perfect life, perfect relationship, or perfect children**.

BUT what if you could live a life filled with passion, love, and excitement, minus the stress of perfection?

This book will show you, it's absolutely possible to have your dream life, relationship, and family. But, only once you realize you're in this journey together, as a couple.

We want to create a journey filled with laughter and fun too.

I've been with my husband for nearly 30 years, so everything I teach comes from true blue experience. In my teachings, I only implement the best of what I've learned from the 'professionals'. If it is based on theory and doesn't have proof of working in the real world (versus the clinical world), you'll never see it in anything I produce. I have a no bullsh*t system. We are all too busy for theoretical hypothesis. This book will help save you time and energy while also helping you to achieve the incredible life you are ready to live.

You will learn how to build the life you want, while taking out the overwhelming complications. It's structured around reinforcing and improving your relationship.

This book will help you learn to:

- Create your dream life

- Look and feel sexier/more confident

- Increase romance & passion

- Crush obstacles

- End the fighting cycle

- Crack through the mental financial ceiling

- Develop a blueprint for success

- Make the positive changes permanent

- Most importantly...*Live a life filled with fun and excitement!*

How to Use This Book

First, take our Live Sexy Relationship Assessment to find out where your relationship is strong and where is needs attention. The quiz will only take about 3 minutes and is quite enlightening. You can find it here: www. LiveSexyQuiz.com.

Read chapters 1 and 2, completing all the exercises fully. This will give you a good foundation, preparing you for the rest of the book. These are important steps, so take your time and submerse yourself in the exercises.

Once you have finished that, start on the chapter that addresses the area of your relationship that needs the most work according to your assessment. Then, feel free to explore the other chapters. Find those that are the most interesting to you and read through the information. Be sure to complete all exercises along the way in order to achieve the strongest transformation.

CHAPTER 1

DREAM TOGETHER. DREAM BIG!

"Create the highest, grandest vision possible for your life, because you become what you believe."

—Oprah

All of us have dreams and aspirations, however, too often life jumps in front of those plans and takes us off course. The beauty of having a life partner is that two is more powerful and way more exciting than one. This chapter is going to inspire you to dream again and help you create a plan to attain the amazing life you want to live. It's much easier than you suspect and when both of you are invested in it, the process of getting there is exhilarating.

Be Clear on What Your Dreams Are

It's essential that you be very clear on what your dreams are. It's impossible to go after your dreams if you can't see them perfectly. A clear vision creates excitement, keeps you focused, and allows you to develop a plan of action to get there. The Wright brothers would never have been able to fly, if they weren't clear on what they wanted to accomplish.

Do not allow self-limiting beliefs to interrupt your brainstorming. Later, we will work on how to achieve your goals and make them obtainable versus getting stuck because they feel too overwhelming

Remember, if not you...then who?? Don't give your dream away. You *deserve* to live them.

Some questions to ask yourself:

- What are your core values?

- What is most important to you?

- Where do you want to live—near water, on a vineyard, in the mountains?

- Do you want to be closer to family?

- What type of home would you like to live in? Be very specific here—Nantucket style, Victorian, Mid-Century Modern, etc. Think of color, shingles or no shingles, porch or no porch.

- What about your career? Is there a company or position you desire? Do you dream of starting your own business? Do you want to remain in your current career but work less? Decrease stress?

- What type of vacations would you like to take? Exotic, educational, Peace Corp, luxury, active.

6

- How do you want to spend your free time? Gardening, skiing, traveling, volunteering.

- What do you want to be remembered for?

Power of Feelings and Emotions

Changing your thoughts using emotional energy has a much greater impact on driving you to success. Emotional energy is the positive, upbeat feelings that drive you. Think about how you'll feel once you attain your goals. What emotions describe it? Will things improve for your family? How will others think of you?

Mira Kirshenbaum, author of, *The Emotional Energy Factor*, states, "When you increase your emotional energy, it's amazing how your dreams become realities."

We all know people with a high emotional energy. They're the ones that can change the feel of a room when they enter it. They exude happiness, passion, and positive energy. Those with high emotional energy face challenges with a 'can do' attitude, focusing on what's possible versus what's not. They reframe a negative into a positive.

Dig for thoughts that excite you and create passion. Avoid statements that involve negativity such as, "I will be less stressed out." It's more helpful to make a statement such as, "When I achieve (insert goal), I will feel (use the emotions you want to feel)." Here's an example: "Once I accomplish working out for 21 days straight, I will feel strong and proud."

7

Don't reach for the crumbs. Go for the cake.

Want a beautiful life? If all you're reaching for is crumbs, piecing them together will never make you a cake. You must take action and be ready when opportunity arises.

Ray Kroc, the man responsible for McDonalds, started as a salesman of milkshake mixers. He noticed how one of his accounts had a formula for doing better than all the rest. Kroc saw an opportunity to scale the business, took action, and the rest is history.

It's also imperative that you keep trying, despite setbacks. Thomas A. Edison "failed" 10,000 times before he perfected the incandescent electric light bulb.

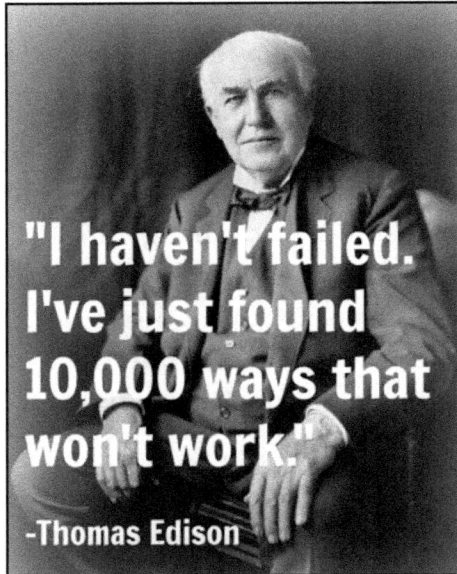

"I haven't failed. I've just found 10,000 ways that won't work."
-Thomas Edison

Don't Allow Perceived Limitations to Stop You

Henry Ford was poor and uneducated. He dreamed of a horseless carriage. He took what tools he had and went to work on creating his vision. And, as we know, he revolutionized the transportation industry; creating an affordable car that could be driven easily. Despite being told countless times how impossible it was, especially based on his lack of education, he had a success mentality. Imagine if he had a failure mentality.

Exercise 1: Dream Big

First:

- Set aside a few hours to work on this with your partner.

- Create an environment that allows your mind to flow. Example: I enjoy listening to background music. I light several candles and establish a positive and mindful atmosphere. A glass of wine can be just the right amount of relaxation to open up the brain.

- Have a pen and paper ready to write out your lists.

Next:

- Both of you write a list of what is most important to you. Think about what your dreams are. Do NOT limit yourself. Write every idea that comes to you. You can pare it down later, but do not allow perceived obstacles or self-limiting thoughts to hold back what you write down.

- What emotions do you feel when you envision yourself living these goals? How does your spouse look at you? What do your friends, family, and associates think of you?

- Compare and circle commonalities. It's okay if you have differences from your partner's, but focus on the commonalities. Remember, this is an exercise to discover what you *both* want. If there is something you strongly desire but your partner does not, write it down separately and re-visit it at a later time to see how it can be incorporated.

- Break down steps to achieve your goals. Brainstorm ideas of how to make your dreams a reality. Who do you know? What are other avenues to get there?

- Write down the perceived obstacles. Really look at those obstacles and think of how to overcome them. Think outside of the 'box.'

  ◊ Example: You want a new career as a social media expert, so you can work from home. The problem is you have no formal background in the field, you are not a young kid, and have no clients. Ideas to get you to this goal: Intern for free for the biggest social media expert you can find. Aid a friend or business that needs social media help in order to start building your resume. Get on email lists of the biggest players in the industry and watch for their seminars.

  Need inspiration? Look at magazines and on the internet. Think back to when you were younger; what were your dreams and visions then?

Make sure to discuss the results together. It's amazing the magic that can happen by simply talking out loud about your dreams. Solutions arise, the dreams become more realistic, and the excitement that you're working together to achieve something great is uplifting. Stay positive. Do NOT be a Debbie Downer and talk about all the reasons why something can't happen. They are simply obstacles. See them this way, and figure out solutions. Remember to have a 'success mentality.' This is the start to changing your thought patterns.

> ***Trick to crushing obstacles.*** I close my eyes and imagine a bridge with giant boulders on it; each boulder representing a challenge or obstacle. In my mind's eye, I see myself approaching and shoving each giant rock off the bridge. It symbolizes to me, that I have the power to simply push them out of my way, to get to where I want to go.

CHAPTER 2

IT'S ALL IN THE ATTITUDE

"Attitude is a little thing that makes a big difference."

—Winston Churchill

This is a busy, active chapter but what you'll learn will affect your entire life and future. Remember, you design your own future by making a conscious choice of what you want. Therefore, what you desire has to be extremely clear. You will be reinforcing your vision in this chapter, beginning to make it more tangible. You'll learn how a positive mental attitude can transform your life.

Next, I'll teach you the practice of 'Positive Affirmations.' You'll learn that 'fear of failure' keeps us from achieving our dreams and how to overcome this mental challenge. Finally, we'll look at how meditation and hypnotherapy work to clear our minds and increase productivity, change behaviors, and ultimately help us see things better.

Effect of a Positive vs. Negative Mental Attitude

Do you have a tendency to criticize others? When something doesn't go your way are you a finger-pointer? Have you said, "Things were out of my control," instead of taking responsibility? Do you see the glass half-empty or half-full?

The way you answered the questions above may be an indicator of your mental attitude. Gossiping, blaming others, not looking for the positive in situations, are all examples of negative thinking. Every one of us is guilty of this to some extent BUT the more we take responsibility and the more we look for positives in situations; the healthier, more resilient, less stressed, and more successful we'll become. There is an abundance of scientific studies that prove the importance of a positive attitude and the ill effects of negative thoughts.

> **Here is a link to a tool to measure your attitude.**
>
> It's focused more for the work place but will still give you some insight into what your tendencies lean toward. **http://www.mindtools.com/pages/article/newTCS_89.htm**

Neuroplasticity: Control and Change Our Brain

The great news is: we have the ability to transform our thought patterns through Neuroplasticity. This science shows the brain alters and changes continually throughout our entire life. What this means is, regardless of our current belief system, we can manipulate our brain to change habits, beliefs, and behaviors.

An example of this is a person who has always believed they're terrible at math. He can come to believe and make it a reality, that math is simple for him. This also includes a 'self-fulfilling prophecy'. The Urban Dictionary defines it as *positive or negative expectations about circumstances, events, or people that may affect a persons behavior toward them in a manner that he or she (unknowingly) creates situations in which those expectations are fulfilled.*

Neuroplasticity can step in to transform our belief system so you create the 'self-fulfilling prophecy' you desire.

Another example is income. Most of us have a pre-set, unconscious belief of how much money we can earn. I came from a middle-class family. My father was a high school teacher and my mother a stay-at-home mom. My father spoke often of the greed of the 'rich' and how unrealistic it was to gain extreme wealth. His beliefs, subconsciously, set a financial ceiling in my mind. That ceiling held me back from becoming wealthy. I never wanted to be 'greedy,' therefore, I should never be wealthy, was my thought. See how this works? It wasn't until I came to this realization and learned the techniques I'll teach you, that I was able to overcome this limit.

In his widely-acclaimed book, *The Brain That Changes Itself: Stories of Personal Triumph from the Frontiers of Brain Science*, Norman Doidge M.D. states that the brain has the ability to rewire itself and/or form new neural pathways, as long as we do the work. Just like exercise, the work requires repetition and activity to reinforce new learning.

How to Use Positive Affirmations

What is a 'positive affirmation?' These are positive statements that describe a desired situation, which are often repeated, until they get impressed on the subconscious mind. Affirmations are our self-talk; what we tell ourselves and believe as truth.

The practice of affirmations pushes the subconscious mind to take action and work to make the positive statement become reality. We will use positive affirmations to create the 'new truth' that we decide to believe.

Exercise 2: Positive Affirmation

Step 1:

Write out your most important positive affirmation (PA). I suggest focusing on only one or two in the beginning. Think of what you want to change most to create a healthy, passionate life. Do you need to change the way you think of your partner or yourself? Be willing to let go of the past. You are on a journey to attaining your dream life with your partner; you MUST think positively and erase or replace the negative to manifest your goals. Negative thoughts only hold us back.

Rules for Writing your Positive Affirmation:

• Write in present tense.

- Focus on what you want, **not** on what you do not want.

- Focus on you and what you can do for yourself.

Step 2:

Write it on a sticky note and post it in a place that you look at every day, like your mirror.

- Say it to yourself at least 5 times per day. You can change the wording a bit, but be sure you are keeping the same message.

- Look at yourself in the mirror while saying your positive affirmation.

- Use positive body language. Accentuate your message through your hands and arms. Be grandiose while expressing your affirmation. Embrace your inner Mick Jagger.

- Say it 1st thing in the morning and last thing before going to sleep.

Fear of Failure

We often fear doing something new because we don't want to fail. This simple fact holds us hostage from achieving the lives we want to live. The truth is, we can do most anything if we take action, stop negative thinking, and shift our perceptions of the truth about our abilities.

Action step: Force yourself to stop thinking about reasons you can't do something, even if you don't feel brave or capable. Each time you face a fear it becomes easier to overcome other fears/challenges.

Cognitive Reframing: When a negative thought enters your mind, discipline yourself to replace the negative thought with a positive one about your abilities instead. Then take small actions every day toward achieving your goal or desired change.

Review the boulder exercise from the introduction to gain power over your fears.

The Power of Meditation and Hypnotherapy

Meditation has been around for centuries but it wasn't until recently that it's been brought into the mainstream. We have finally caught on to the wonderful benefits it brings!

If insanely successful people, such as Oprah Winfrey, Russell Simmons, Arianna Huffington, and countless Fortune 500 execs are practicing it, there must be value in it.

Ray Dalio, the billionaire founder of Bridgewater Associates, aka the world's largest hedge fund firm, stated, "Meditation more than anything in my life was the biggest ingredient of whatever success I've had."

How much would your life improve if you could experience the following every day:

- Increased memory

- Enhanced creativity

- Ability to think clearer

- Greater joy

- Increased confidence

- Boosted awareness of your purpose and meaning

- Expanded intuition—trusting your gut more

- Higher level of emotional resilience

- Lower stress level

- Enhanced productivity

Exercise 3: Meditation

It's very simple but does take practice. Try to set aside five minutes a day to do this exercise. Take a deep breath and let your mind empty of all thoughts. Sit with your back straight in a chair; breathe comfortably while you focus on your breathing. You can even do this from bed, before rising for the day. However, sitting up does allow the breathing to flow a bit better. I, personally, imagine a white, swirling cloud entering my body as I breathe in. I imagine it traveling throughout my body, starting at my head and going down from there. Then, everything is cleaned out as I exhale. You don't have to say or do anything during this exercise, just set an intention for your day or visualize how you want your day to go in your mind's eye.

> *Hint:* When you encounter something in your day or life that causes extreme stress or anxiety practice this five-minute exercise. You'll be

amazed at how much easier it becomes to deal with your issues.

Benefits of Hypnotherapy

I'll admit, I thought of hypnotherapy merely as a pseudoscience and was extremely skeptical of this 'mind-altering' practice ... until I tried it. It was the most profound, most helpful, most life-changing experience I've had. I was alert and aware of everything being said to me during it. My experience was nothing like what you see from 'stage performances' of hypnotherapy. In general, you tell the hypnotherapist what you want to achieve—weight loss, overcoming phobias, control over your emotions, increasing mindset for success, etc. The hypnotherapist helps you get into a relaxed state, at which point, they use your exact words and goals to reach your subconscious. The first time I went, it was so successful that I became a bit overzealous, in what I wanted to achieve. It was fairly easy to consciously alter my behavior and thoughts to reach the desired effect.

I have been to a few hypnotherapists now and seem to have the best results from one particular practitioner. It is important to find a respected and knowledgeable hypnotherapist that you feel comfortable with.

How Hypnotherapy Works

Contrary to what has been depicted in the old horror movies, you are not under the control of a 'master' that wants you to do horrendous acts. In fact, those in a hypnotic state are not asleep. They're actually hyper attentive, and super focused because they tune out the stimuli around them. It's been characterized as daydreaming or extreme relaxation. Once you are in a hypnotic trance, you are more receptive to suggestion.

An important point to know is that if the practitioner states something you do not *want* to accept you will consciously reject it.

I believe hypnotherapy is incredibly instrumental in creating positive change that My 'Live Sexy Accelerated Relationship System' incorporates a series of hypnotherapy CD's to reinforce everything that is taught. I feel it's an important tool in maintaining the changes you desire.

CHAPTER 3

ACHIEVING YOUR
ULTIMATE LIFE

"If you don't know where you're going, you'll
end up someplace else."

— Yogi Berra

Now that you've figured out what you want in life, it's
time to plan how to get there. If you want to succeed,
it's essential to set goals. Without goals you lack focus
and direction. Goal setting allows you to take control
of your life's direction, and it also provides you a
benchmark for determining whether you are succeeding
or need to establish a different path. On top of that, the
act of writing out your goals reinforces their tangibility.
When planning your goals, make sure to include: where
you want to be financially, your job or career changes
(if applicable), vacations, and big purchases (i.e. pool,
home, remodel, etc).

Set SMART Goals

The 'SMART' goal system is the system I use to simplify my own goal setting. I use the acronym to help me remember the rules of goal setting. To have powerful goals, they should be designed to be SMART.

There are many variations of what SMART stands for, but the essence is this—goals should be:

- **S**pecific

- **M**easurable

- **A**ttainable

- **R**elevant

- **T**ime Bound

I recommend setting up a chart and post it on your wall, so you can see your progress. You'll probably need three separate charts to differentiate your personal and your partner's goals, and a chart for your mutual goals/dreams. There may be some overlap between the charts, which just means when you achieve your goal, you get to check off the goal in two separate areas.

Set Specific Goals

Your goal must be clear and well defined. Vague or generalized goals are not helpful because they don't provide sufficient direction. Remember, you need goals to show you the way. Each goal should be able to answer these questions: Who, What, Where, When, Why. To get where you want to go, make it as easy as you can by defining where you want to end up.

Example: General goal "To feel closer to my spouse." A specific goal would be more like this, "Plan date nights two times per month and say one thing daily of how much we appreciate the other."

Set Measurable Goals

Include precise amounts, dates, and so on in your goals so you can measure your degree of success. If your goal is simply defined as, "To save money," how will you know when you have been successful? Without a way to measure your success you miss out on the celebration that comes with knowing you have actually achieved something.

Example: Goal, "To pay off my credit card within 12 months." From here, work backwards to decide how much you need to be saving per month and what you'll be cutting out to attain your goal.

Set Attainable Goals

This acronym stresses that you make 'attainable goals,' in order to avoid demoralizing yourself and eroding your confidence. I'm careful with this one because we are way more capable of achievement, than we allow ourselves to be. Everything this book is teaching you is about pushing your limits and conquering fears/obstacles to attain the dream life you deserve and want.

My suggestion is to set large goals, *but* break them down into smaller goals that ultimately lead to the large goal. This will create momentum and confidence. By setting realistic, yet challenging goals, you hit the balance you need. These are the types of goals that require you to "raise the bar," and they bring the greatest personal satisfaction.

Set Relevant Goals

Goals should be relevant to the direction you want your life and career to take. By keeping goals aligned with this, you'll develop the focus you need to get ahead and do what you want.

Set Time-Bound Goals

A goal needs to have a time frame. With no time frame tied to it, there's no sense of urgency. If you want to lose 10 lbs.: when do you want to lose it by? "Someday" won't work. But, if you anchor it within a timeframe, "by June 1st", then you've set your unconscious mind into motion to begin working on the goal. Another example is that you want to change careers. Set the date you want to be in your new career by. Work backwards from that point, setting smaller goals that need to be attained to reach your new career.

Example: Your Goal: Completely shift from current career to being a full-time Social Media Expert by December 1st, 2016.

Sub goals:

• Spend 10 hours a week learning social media: *immediate*

- Become intern for a social media expert: *April 1st, 2015*

- Gain social media presence: start blog, Facebook page, and Google + page: *May 1st, 2015*

- Do pro-bono work to build resume and testimonials: *June 1st, 2015*

- Go to 3 top social media or marketing conventions: *throughout 2015—2016*

- Make 3 strong connections at each event

Chart It Out

Once you have everything written out, it's time to chart out your goals. My clients have found higher success setting 90-day goals because it helps to maintain focus and motivation. It also makes it easier to pivot if something changes. I also recommend setting 12 month, 3 year, 5 year, and 10-year goals, to know what you're working toward and have a bigger vision. Not to freak you out but it's also a good idea to plan out how you want retirement to look, so you're clear on what needs to be done to achieve your ultimate retirement.

Now, use a planner to ensure you take action steps weekly, even daily, to get you where you want to be. It's important to make this a habit, so review your necessary action steps every morning or the night before. This has been a HUGE needle turner for me. Every Monday morning, I break out my Z'Luxe Life Action Planner and write out my plan for the week. I chunk it down by each day. It maintains focus, discipline, and you'll be amazed by how much you get done, simply by having a list to refer to daily.

At times it can feel you're making little progress but I promise if you religiously commit to taking small action steps daily, or even weekly, things will change.

Make a note on your calendar to review your goals every ninety days in order to keep them fresh on your mind, make sure you're staying on track, and make the necessary adjustments. **Celebrate your wins too!** If you are staying the course to achieve a particular goal, that's a win. Go reward yourself!

You see how that works? It's absolutely do-able. You simply need a blue print action plan to get there.

*Check out my Z'Luxe Life Action Planner, which breaks the goals up into 90 day increments. It guides you to write your daily and weekly goals so you can attain your 90 day goals easily. **www.ZluxeLife.com/programs/***

CHAPTER 4

WHO IS THAT IN YOUR BED?

"Love is our true destiny. We do not find the meaning of life by ourselves alone—we find it with another."

—Thomas Merton

Why Even Bother Reconnecting?

Has your relationship gotten to the point where you think maybe you'll be happier without your partner? Does it feel like you've gotten in such a deep rut that digging out feels nearly impossible? Many couples experience this hopeless feeling at some point, however, it's absolutely possible to change it around and find happiness again. Just start small and simple. The compound effect will pay off.

Here are a few reasons why it's worth your time to find each other again:

Long-term married couples...

- *Live longer.* A UCLA study found that people in generally excellent health were 88 percent more likely to die over the 8-year study period if they were single.

- *Earn 22% more money.* A Virginia Commonwealth University study found that married men earn 22 percent more than they're similarly experienced but single colleagues.

- *Build trust & confidence*

- *Quicker to recover from life's downfalls*

- *Take more risks = higher achievements!*

- *Socially happier*

Issues to Watch Out For

When you're together with the same person for an extended period of time, expect to have ups and downs. That's life! It's how quickly you recognize, deal, and effectively resolve your issues that make a successful healthy relationship.

Some of the most common issues leading couples to disconnect (of course, this is not a comprehensive list) and create distance from one another are: anxiety from work, demands of raising children, caring for elderly parents, relationship boredom. The problem with these types of issues is that they creep in slowly and manifest until they take over. Often you're unaware, or too consumed, to clearly see the full picture, until it becomes a monumental or disastrous situation. Are you simply bored in your relationship from being together for so long? Is there nothing new, or exciting?

Built up grudges are another thing that happens over time. It can start small, maybe some name-calling, not listening to your partner, or not sharing in household chores. Grievances that don't get dealt with can cause a withdrawal and disconnect in a relationship.

Suggestions to reconnect:

Simple touch. This is effective without being too overt, especially if you have a deep disconnected. Touch your partner's hand or back lightly. Try caressing their hair just a bit. Make it a practice to do these small actions at least once a day.

Listen to your partner. When your partner is talking or telling you something, be one hundred percent present. Show that you're listening, make the eye contact and nod your head.

There's a well-respected psychologist and relationship therapist named Dr. John Gottman. His book, *The Relationship Cure*, talks about a concept he calls 'turning in versus turning out.' He illustrates how simple body language impacts communication. The act of turning in to your partner when they're talking, no matter what they're talking about, can seem inconsequential to you, however, you are showing that you're listening and making a positive response to what they are saying. No matter what they are talking about, turn toward them and make a comment in response (be positive) to show that you are listening and that you do have interest in what they're saying. When you consistently turn away and don't verbally respond, you are sending a message that you're ignoring, not really listening, or have no interest in your partner. This creates a huge amount of damage in the relationship. *Be aware.* 'Turn in' and make a positive verbal response, as often as you can.

In the past, if I was working on something important and my husband started to tell me something he was reading in the newspaper, I would definitely not turn toward him and I might even ignore his words. Over time, his resentment built, which he illustrated one day when he told me, "You are not the same! You are always focused on work." I now realize how easy it is to change this perception AND how detrimental it is to a relationship. Now, it only takes me a second to turn toward him and make a response - done! If I'm doing something that takes my full attention, I will turn toward him and acknowledge his comment by gently saying something like, "What? That's crazy! Hun, I'm almost done with this project but need a half-hour to stay totally focused and then I'll be free." This shows him I'm listening and interested but need some time not to be interrupted.

He and I have spoken about how he was feeling - basically, that I was being an inconsiderate bitch (my words - not his). I expressed my need to stay focused on my task or else I get completely lost. We now understand each other's thoughts and needs. When I mention I need 'to stay focused,' he doesn't take it personally because he knows how easily distracted I am (ADD is a definite possibility). My action of turning toward him and responding reminds him how important he is to me. Simple!

Look within yourself. What are you doing to create distance? Are you the one experiencing the withdrawal? Are you pulling back? Are you turning away and not turning in? Pay attention to what you're doing and how your actions and your words may be contributing to that disconnect. Make it a point to change that around.

Establish routines. Routines can be surprisingly helpful to a relationship. Simple things; like drinking coffee, reading the newspaper together, going to the farmer's market every Sunday, watching a favorite TV show weekly, can provide easy but beneficial routines for you and your partner to look forward to.

> Tip: If one person cannot be there to watch the favorite show, record it to watch together at a more convenient time. Make it a date!

Small dates. Many couples focus only on the big date night, which can feel overwhelming. Small dates are just as important and simpler to make happen. An example of a small date could be going on a quiet drive where there are very few distractions. Some other ideas: going to the beach, going on a hike, or to an old favorite spot. Try to do something where there's an activity so you're not just sitting there feeling uncomfortable, not knowing how to talk to one another. Look for dates where you can walk, dance, play, or interact. Playing cards or a game can break the ice and be a lot of fun.

Going to dinner, at this point, might be a bit uncomfortable, particularly if the communication doesn't come easily. A movie and then going out after for coffee, dessert, or a glass of wine, can be a more successful date. Use the movie as the source of discussion. It gives you something to connect with. Just be mindful of listening, and of turning in and responding. You don't have to agree, but be respectful and engage. That's what this whole date is about.

Practice gratitude. Another action to help you reconnect is practicing gratitude. Write out ten things that you are grateful for with your partner. It could be as simple as your partner picking up the newspaper and bringing it to you in the morning, they help you with the laundry, or they help you with the dishes. The knowledge that they're on your side when work or life gets rough is incredibly comforting. He greets you when you come home from work, etc.

Really take the time to think about this one because there are probably a number of things that without your partner would make your life not as happy. What would your life look like without these actions your partner provides?

Those who express and practice gratitude on a regular basis are happier, have a more positive outlook, feel more alive, sleep better, express more compassion and kindness, and are healthier. Who doesn't want all that ... and it's free!!

Quick Tips on Reconnecting

- Deal with issues when they're small
- Simple touch
- Turn in versus turning out
- Establish routines/traditions
- Small dates
- Gratitude!

CHAPTER 5

LIVE SEXY—GET YOUR MOJO BACK!

"Our deepest fear is not that we are inadequate. Our deepest fear is that we are powerful beyond measure. It is our light, not our darkness, that most frightens us. We ask ourselves, 'Who am I to be brilliant, gorgeous, talented, fabulous?' Actually, who are you not to be?"

—Marianne Williamson

Debi Silber MS, RD, WHC™, FDN, The Mojo Coach®, President of Lifestyle Fitness, Inc., and founder of www.TheMojoCoach.com is a recognized health, weight loss, fitness, wellness, lifestyle and self-improvement expert. Specifically, she's a Registered Dietitian with a Master's degree in Nutrition, a certified Personal Trainer, and Whole Health Coach, has two certifications in pre- and post-natal fitness with specialty recognition in weight loss and weight maintenance, and is a Functional Diagnostic

Nutrition Practitioner. She's also a working mom with 4 kids, 6 dogs, and has been married to her husband Adam for 23+ years.

Debi's branded The Mojo Coach® because she's led thousands of clients to achieve their ultimate body, mind, image, and lifestyle; inspiring them to "get their mojo back," and helping them transform into their personal and professional best. She's a master at showing others how to create a lean, fit body, radiant health, soaring confidence, endless energy, rewarding relationships, financial abundance, a dynamic image, charismatic style, and an optimistic outlook.

How Debi Came to be 'The Mojo Coach'

Spoken from Debi.

It was 2008 and I had a great, full-time business as a dietician I was also a personal trainer, and had a Masters in nutrition. My clients were getting lean and getting healthy. At the time, I, also, had a husband, home, four kids, and only four dogs then.

Unfortunately, I also had some toxic relationships, and chronic stress. I was trying to be everything to everyone all the time. I started to get sick. First, it was symptoms, but I was just too busy, so I blew them off. Then the symptoms turned into conditions, and, again, I was too busy. I simply didn't have the time.

Then my conditions grew to illnesses, and eventually full-blown disease. Your body will speak louder and louder until you pay attention, and, well, that got my attention. Things actually got so bad that I had to give up my entire business, with clients I loved, because I couldn't get out of bed. You name it, I had it. I should have been a picture of health. I was a health expert, but I was anything but healthy.

It hit me that it had to have something to do with my mindset, my lifestyle, and the toxic relationships I was in. I had surgery. During my healing process, I studied to become a whole health coach. That's a health expert, trained to teach how your lifestyle creates either health or wellness, or illness and disease. While I was going through that program, I learned that, yes, my mindset, the stress I was under, and the relationships I had were really at the root of it all.

So, I thought, "Well, since I have the eating and exercise part down, what would happen if I changed those other things?" And I did.

Over the next nine months, I healed from everything. I got my mojo back. Started working with clients, but this time in a very different way. *They* started getting their mojo back. Soon my clients were calling me "The Mojo Coach," and my complete transformation system was born. And ever since, I've been on this mission to share it with as many people as I can.

Have you lost your Mojo?

You know you have your Mojo when you're feeling at the top of your game: feeling good in your own skin. A person with mojo feels confident and sexy. A person who has lost their mojo may feel threatened, jealous, uncomfortable, and/or insecure. We all have these emotions that creep up from time to time, but, for the most part, a person who has their mojo feels good physically, emotionally, and mentally.

When your mojo is gone, it feels like you lost your rhythm. You've lost the grip and the handle on those healthy habits that you had.

Every single thing we do brings us only one of two directions: further or closer to the body, health, lifestyle that we want, and the energy that we want. When we've lost our mojo, it's likely that we have taken too many steps in the wrong direction. We are moving away from what it is that we desire.

Here are 3 quick tips to get your mojo back:

- **Exercise**: This is the one thing that we can control and when we give ourselves that gift, we feel so much better, despite how chaotic the rest of the world around us may be.

- **Mindset**: When we lose our confidence, very often it's because we have old beliefs that simply don't serve us. We have that negative self-talk in our head, and it's taking up all this room. This can really work for you or against you. I invite you to question every belief you have, and if it doesn't serve you, consider letting it go.

- **Relationships**: Check your relationships. Who are you spending time with? Your relationships are not only good and bad for you mentally and emotionally, but physically, too. Negative, toxic, critical, judgmental people, can actually suppress our immune system. When thinking about what may be a major confidence killer, think of the people around you. Are they supportive, loving, and nurturing? Do they make you feel good? Do they encourage you to up your game?

Or, on the other hand, do you feel drained, spent, depleted, exhausted, like you need a nap? Do you feel worse after spending time with them? Your relationships have so much to do with your confidence.

Consequences from Lack of Confidence

Pay attention to how you dress, the way you move, and the way you interact or don't interact. The opportunities you pass by, because you didn't have the confidence to take them on.

Confidence affects every aspect of life. I see this in the work I do. Someone will tell me, "Oh, I always have these (unhealthy) relationships, and I get taken advantage of, and this happens and that happens." The truth is, *we* write the script for how people treat us. And, with a lack of confidence, you write a very different script than someone who truly possesses confidence.

Often, clients will want to work on what they can do *with that person* to improve the situation. *Wrong!* I always start by having them work on themselves, because the stronger and better you feel, the better *everything* is. You radiate a certain energy, and the energy is very different when you're not feeling your best, or when you're not at the top of your game.

Superwoman/Superman Crash and Burn

Many people wonder how I balance having 4 kids, 6 dogs, a husband, and a career. Well, I know it's easy to get caught up with the whole Superwoman/Superman thing, and that's actually one of the things that had me crash the first time. But, I can assure you, keeping that Super person cape on is a recipe for Super-stress, and eventually, disaster. You have to let it go.

Here are a few things I learned to do. Stay true to your priorities, and simply let the rest *go*. When you try to be perfect in all areas, first of all, *who cares*, and secondly, why is that? Who set the bar that high? Who are you comparing yourself to? It's not that you're unable to do these things. *You're magnificent! You can do everything.* But, what's the benefit of this level of perfection? It's impossible to maintain and feel healthy.

The first thing I did for myself was redefine "perfect." Then, I got rid of perfect altogether because *who cares?*

The second thing I did, was really discover what my priorities were, and I let the rest *go*. For example, it's very important that I have healthy meals for my family, but who's got time? So, I make everything five ingredients or less. That's my rule. It's simplifying.

Another thing I did was redefine the work-life balance. I just don't believe that exists. We can't be balanced in all areas. It's impossible. Imagine you have 100% of energy. That's all you have. Then, let's say you're focused on work, but, meanwhile, 50% of your energy is going towards your work, and 50% is thinking about all the things that you need to do at home, or with the kids, or with your partner ... I realized when I did that, I kind of stunk across the board.

Instead, I said, "Well, what would happen if I was 100% in the space I'm in?" Just that small shift allowed me to be much more present in each space. When I'm working, I can be 100% present for a client, or when I'm speaking, or whatever I'm doing. When I'm with my kids, I can be 100% present with them.

That tiny shift made things so much easier. Like I said before, take a look at your priorities, and really let the rest *go*. It's just not that important.

There's a freedom you feel in the end, because now you can do what's bringing you closer to what you want, and let the rest *go*.

When you try to do it all, you absolutely dilute your power.

Are Your Food Choices Making You Sick and Tired?

Food has so much to do with our energy, our confidence, and the way we look and feel. Whole, real, nutrient dense foods give our body what it needs.

When making food choices, ask yourself, "Is this going to really fuel and energize me, or is this going to slow me down?" Highly processed, nutrient void, packaged foods are doing very little to help you, but they are wreaking havoc on your health and your waistline.

#1 Food To Avoid

There are a handful of foods that keep you from prancing around in a bikini, being spontaneous, having confidence, or feeling good in your skin. When you replace those foods with ones that actually give you energy, you soar. Your body finds its most comfortable natural weight, cravings decline, and you feel great.

The quickest way to sabotage yourself is with sugar. There is no way I could accomplish all I do every day if I was loaded down with sugar.

Poor food choices are responsible for anything from obesity to depression, anxiety, skin issues, digestive issues, and a lack of energy.

Stop Counting Calories

I never talk about calories. I used to, but I've learned that counting calories keeps you in the diet mentality. What we're creating is a healthy, permanent lifestyle. Also, we now know that a calorie of one food is not necessarily equivalent to another.

The Fat Switch

Imagine you had a fat switch. There are some foods that essentially turn that fat switch on and there are some that turn it off. It has very little to do with counting calories. The true question is where are those calories coming from—highly processed foods, sugary beverages, or healthy, whole foods?

Side note: Professor of Medicine, Richard J. Johnson, in his book, The Fat Switch, says sugar is the main culprit of activating the fat switch. Foods rich in fructose result in loss of appetite control and reduced energy.

Calories are a unit of energy, so what's behind that calorie? What does the food choice do when it's within you? Is it fueling your organs and systems? Is it flooding you with insulin and doing damage?

It's not about the calories. It's absolutely about the food choices. None of my clients worry about calories at all. When you're eating healthy fats, good quality proteins, and flooding yourself with nutrients, just what your body craves, you won't be hungry. You're satisfied, thus this new healthier lifestyle is easier.

Think about it. When you're dieting and you're eating smaller portions of nutrient void food, stuff that doesn't offer you much benefit, you're hungry all the time. You're obsessed with food and cravings are high. There's also a good chance your skin and digestive system are acting up, and it's most likely not bringing you to the weight you want. Eventually you quit and possibly go nuts.

Fitness—Are You a Professional Couch Potato?

My best recommendation for those who may not have exercised in a while is super simple. Just start. Think about it, if you've done nothing, and all of a sudden you commit to waking up a little earlier and putting in ten minutes. That's awesome! That's ten minutes more than you've done before.

Also, think of what you can do throughout the day to move you closer to what you want. Here's an example: I realized I was sitting too much in my office; so, I got rid of my office chair. Now I pace when I'm on the phone and move much more. It is little adjustments, like this, that change your lifestyle.

As far as a fitness program, just begin. Make sure to always get your doctor's approval first.

Long Workouts Are So Yesterday

I work out 20 to 25 minutes every day. That's it! I'm in better shape now after four kids than I was in my thirties.

I want to find all my old clients and apologize to them for the long drawn out cardio sessions. The latest studies shows those long sessions are not healthy for us. They flood us with cortisol, the stress hormone. One of the things cortisol will do is drive the fat storage right to your middle.

What I do is high intensity interval training. You can do this in so many ways based on your fitness level. Design it based on what you enjoy.

Stop Accepting Where You Are

Many people I encounter have the mentality that, "I've let some real unhealthy behaviors and habits get in my way and slow me down. But, you know what, I'm good where I am right now, because it's not my fault. I didn't know better; I didn't have the skills, or tools, etc." For these reasons, we allow ourselves to accept where we are.

What I find a lot of people do is they accept where they are as a reason not to change. This can happen for a number of reasons. I notice with some people that there is a benefit for staying overweight. Although they know it's not healthy, they have concerns over what happens if they become fit, lean, and have a sexy body. Are they ready for the attention? Will there be different expectations? These changes are enough to shake us up and keep us put.

We need to know the reasons why we're accepting where we are, and then, from there, take that step to move on.

#1—Create Awareness

Clients will come to me and say, "Deb, I don't get it. I lose twenty, thirty pounds, and I don't know what happens. I just start gaining it back. I've been to every nutritionist and dietician. What's going on?"

Of course, I'll look at their food and many other things. But then I'll hit on something like relationships, and I'll say, "What happens when you lose twenty-five, thirty pounds? How did your husband react to you?" The responses are interesting. All of a sudden you'll see the deer in headlights look, and it could be something like, "You know what? He gets threatened, jealous, insecure, so I just don't want to rock the boat. It's easier this way." Or, "Oh, my God, he doesn't leave me alone. It's easier this way."

Another client said, "Debi, I don't get it. I lose twenty pounds, and I keep sabotaging myself. I don't know what's going on." This time it wasn't about relationships.

She was a professional comedian. I asked her, "Can you be funny and look good too?" She was stumped. Her reply, "Oh my gosh, I think that's exactly what I'm doing. I don't think I can be funny and sexy, too." Eventually, she came to realize that yes, of course, she could do both successfully.

Find Your Why

Physically, why are you where you are, and why do you want to change it? These two questions are important but it is even more important for you to discover the why behind these two questions.

When I ask these questions to my clients, I always get, "Because I want to feel good." You and everyone else want that BUT what is the real big motivator?

Here's how you find it. Ask yourself *why* and answer with, "So I can..." and see what shows up. "So I can fit into different clothes." Don't stop there. "So I can..." and keep probing, until you hit on the deeply personal reason. That's your *why*.

Maintaining Your Mojo

Once you establish your why, keep that at the top of your mind, and commit to making it a way of life. This way, when you fall off, you'll just get back on. The only difference between someone who maintains a healthy lifestyle for life, and the person who falls off the wagon, is the point when they get back on?

We talked about perfection earlier. Perfection is a straight line. Imagine, a wavy line. To me that's perfect. A little up, a little down, go a little crazy ... then, get back on. That's it! You can do it for life.

Quick Tips to Get Your Mojo Back

- Exercise

- Positive mindset

- Healthy relationships

- Build confidence

- Avoid Super-Person mentality

- Be 100% present

- Eat healthy, whole foods

- Avoid sugar

- Be aware of what you're accepting

- Find your 'why'

CHAPTER 6

COMMUNICATION THAT WORKS!

"Speak when you are angry ... and you'll make the best speech you'll ever regret."

—Laurence Peters

Wonder why you may feel disconnected from one another? Do you sense that your partner has shut down their feelings for you or vice a versa? Hint—it didn't happen overnight. The good news is these issues can be repaired. Keep reading, even if you feel your relationship does not have the above problems because there's a lot to learn to maintain healthy communication.

While reading the 4 Don'ts and 5 Do's, notice which ones pertain to you. When you are acting out one of the 4 Don'ts how do you feel? Often the perpetrator thinks it's not a big deal, thus continuing the behavior, until it escalates into huge problems. The biggest concern with the 4 Don'ts is that it causes a sneaky, slow, destruction to the relationship. The resentment, anger, loss of confidence, unhappiness, build over time and often without notice, until one or both partners finally shut off their feelings for the other.

Control and Power

The basis for most arguments derives from the desire for control and power. Unfortunately, the results are typically a win/lose or lose/lose outcome. It's human nature to believe we are correct and want to sway others to agree with us. My husband and I have had many heated disagreements about raising our kids. Parents love their kids so astronomically and we want to make sure they are raised to the best of our power. What my husband and I have learned is, when we open our minds to listening and understanding the other's perspective, the best solutions are usually a combination of both our ideas. Sometimes one of us is flat out wrong (wowza, that's a tough one to admit), and once we put down our defenses, we are comfortable with the resolution. There's something to be said about the power of two minds.

> TIP: Make discussions your communication goal versus arguments, which accomplish little, other than upsetting each other.

The Love Bank

Yes, we do keep score in relationships. It's generally unconscious but incredibly real. Every positive action you take toward meeting your partner's emotional needs is scored in their internal 'Love Bank.'

Withdrawals from the Love Bank

Every time you perform one of the 4 Don'ts, listed below, points are taken from the bank.

The Good News

Studies show that if you do trip up occasionally, as long as you have plenty of points in the Love Bank, your slip up will most likely be forgiven.

4 Don'ts:

Criticism: This may be the quickest way to ruin a relationship. It often starts small; then, over time, escalates. The criticized person feels controlled, which leads to resentment. The truth of the matter is a person who feels valued will be more open to change, whereas a person who is degraded will resist submitting to the criticizer's wants.

- Avoid attacking your partner's character. Use 'I' statements or constructive feedback. Constructive feedback focuses on how to improve the situation. An example of this is stating, "You've done a great job raising our kids. I think it will be a huge benefit to them that we get them to school on time, every day." (*Actual statement from my husband regarding my consistent ineptness at being timely. Since he said it prefaced with a positive and followed by constructive suggestion, I actually listened and worked on limiting my tardiness.)*

Now imagine he said this instead, "Did you skip clock reading in school because you suck at being on time! Our kids are going to grow up being as irresponsible as you." Guess what my response would be to that? Not only would he fail at getting what he wanted but he'd also have the possibly of a burnt dinner or more likely, no dinner.

- *Disrespect*: Are you a name-caller or do you roll your eyes at your spouse's comments? What about ignoring your partner? Are you known for your sharp tongue, aka sarcasm? If so, it's likely harvesting negative feelings and resentment. Once your partner starts disrespecting back, it becomes a vicious cycle. I'll admit I'm a professional eye-roller. Once I became aware of the harmful implications of my eye-rolls, I realized it was time to shelf it and find a new expertise!

- *Defensiveness*: Listen, hear, and think before responding. It's important to take responsibility for your actions. If your spouse makes a statement that he's tired of the car being messy, take ownership of it. You might say, "I agree. I will make sure the kids and I take all our belongings out after school every day."

Here's another situation that happens in many households: Your partner may comment that she needs more help with the kids. Instead of being defensive by saying, "I already work 50 hours a week and volunteer. I have nothing left!" Responding with something like, "I agree that I could do more. Will it help if I take them to breakfast on Sundays so you can have a break or get other things done?" In the second scenario, you acknowledge her pain and show respect by offering to alleviate her. This goes a long way because this act shows support, love, and giving. Wow, points in the bank!

- *Stonewalling*: The definition of stonewalling is the refusal to communicate or cooperate. Examples of stonewalling include: giving short, vague responses, refusing to answer questions, mumbling, and the silent treatment.

- Here are typical stonewalling phrases:

  ◊ "Leave me alone…"

  ◊ "I'm done talking about it!"

  ◊ "End of discussion."

  ◊ "I don't want to talk about it."

  ◊ "Shut up."

So, What to Do?

The stonewalling tactic, according to Dr. John Gottman's research, is a huge indicator of predicting divorce. The only solution to this is to communicate. Sorry, permanent avoidance won't work long! Note that I said permanent avoidance. Time-outs are okay and suggested when things get too heated, though.

5 Do's

- *Calm Down*: When your heart is beating 90 beats-per-minute, it makes it difficult to think logically. This is the dangerous territory when we say things we regret later. Take a break when you notice things are getting too heated. If you know this is a problem in your relationship, discuss it when things are relaxed. I suggest having a *safety term*, which indicates you need to separate for a time and revisit the issue later. An example of a *safety term* can be "I need 20 minutes," or "CD break" (CD = calm down).

    TIP: This technique works every time for me. Take a deep breath in. When exhaling, say your first and last name. Repeat ten times. This acts as an interrupter for your brain and diffuses the angry feelings.

    TIP #2 for dealing with someone out-of-control: Make this statement, "Please speak more slowly. I want to help." They may not be speaking too quickly but it's another example of a brain interrupter. They are expecting you to respond differently but when you respond with support, you're helping them shift their brain pattern back to a thinking mode.

- *Complain*: Deal with the issue—don't be a doormat. Being complacent to "keep the peace" will result in one person becoming incredibly dominating and the other filled with resentment and a feeling of no control. A way to start a discussion is, "(This action) bothers me because it makes me feel (_____)."

Don't be afraid to use a strong, powerful voice. It's important to set limits and establish respect for each other. This is much different than yelling. A powerful voice is one with control. Yelling and screaming are indicators of lack of control.

- *Speak Non-Defensively*: Don't yell. Start sentences with "I" statements versus "you" statements. "I feel..." "We" statements are also effective. *Example*: "We should have date nights twice a month." Even better: "I would love to spend more quality time with you. To help make our relationship even stronger, let's go on date nights twice a month." Do you see what the second example did? It expressed desire to be with the other; thinking of the future together ("...make our relationship even stronger..."); and a solution. More points in the bank!

- *Validate*: Validation is done by fully listening. This is expressed through our body language, and sharing a reflection of their comment. Listen to what your partner is truly saying – what needs or emotions are they expressing? Is there an underlying message? Ask questions, such as, "Are you saying that it would make your life easier if I help you more with household chores?"

An example of reflection is: "If I understand you correctly, you're saying that if I chipped in more with the chores, it would make your life easier."

Reflection is often referred to as mirroring. If your reflection is on target, follow your statement with your promise, "Now that I'm aware of how much this has been a problem, I will absolutely help more." This shows that you are listening and that their message is important to you. Boom, more points in the bank.

- *Practice!:* It's important for these to become a natural part of your communication, thus, continually practicing and implementing them is the only way to make it habit.

Main Points

- **Build your 'Love Bank'**

- **Take Time-Outs**

- *4 Don'ts*

  ◊ **Criticism**

  ◊ **Disrespect**

  ◊ **Defensiveness**

  ◊ **Stonewalling**

- *5 Do's*

  ◊ **Calm down**

  ◊ **Don't be a doormat**

  ◊ **Use non-defensive statements**

  ◊ **Validate-reflection**

  ◊ **Practice!**

CHAPTER 7

CHEAT SHEET TO THE OPPOSITE SEX

This chapter is an extension of the last chapter about communication.

These are highlighted tips to help gain perspective on how the opposite sex thinks to create understanding and greater happiness for marriage success. Hopefully, it'll help you understand why she's mad again or why he doesn't talk when he gets home.

The book, *Men Are From Mars, Women Are From Venus,* written by John Gray, was a smashing hit because we are often completely confused by the opposite sex. However, once we understand the other sex, the success of our marriage and the success in relationships will improve *and* might even thrive!

Here is a quick list that you should study, and maybe keep in your back pocket, for those moments that makes no sense to you:

What Wives Want:

- *Affirmation of love.* Tell me and show me how much you love me.

- *Understanding & forgiveness.* We can be grumpy and we do make mistakes. It could be a hormone issue. It could also be due to the fact that we have a hard time shutting our brains down leading us to occasional grumpiness.

- *Conversation.* Talk to us about more than just the kids, jobs, or weather. We want to be intellectually stimulated; we want to hear the funny stories the guys secretly talk about ... although, some editing is probably a good idea.

- *Quality Time.* Make us a priority at least once a week.

- *Be Positive.* Too much negativity wears us down and makes you not as sexy.

- *Listen!* Hear us out before you respond. Even when it seems like we're talking about something inconsequential, hear us and acknowledge us positively.

- *Affection and Kindness.* Open the door, say please and thank you. Be kind. Words do hurt and we *might* take them a little too seriously.

- *Compliment Us.* A simple compliment about our abilities, appearance, and intelligence has a huge effect on our confidence and happiness! *Shh ... it may even help you get lucky!*

- *Help Us Out*. Please, please, share in household chores, responsibilities for our children, and simple things, like groceries.

  FACT: Men who help in household chores do enjoy better sex lives. Yes, there have been scientific studies about this!

What Husbands Want:

- *Affection.* Hold our hands, touch us, kiss our cheeks. Flirt with us.

- *Support & Believe in Us*. It's our instinct to want to protect and provide for the family. Reassure us that we are doing well and that you appreciate what we do.

- *10-Minute Rule*. When we get home, we need 10 minutes to ourselves. We welcome you greeting us, but please wait to tell us about problems or needs until we have our decompression time.

- *Acceptance*. Stop trying to change us. We will never be the same as you ... and truthfully, would you really want that? Focus on our positives.

- *Less Chatter*. We want to listen to you but it's a fact that our hearing shuts off after 6 minutes of chatting. Yes, selective hearing is a proven fact. Sorry!

- *Respect*. Avoid the eye roll. Listen and be mindful of how you respond to me. A positive attitude is as important to me as it is to you.

- *Companionship.* Be my cheerleader, lover, and friend.

- *Sex.* I know this can seem like a chore sometimes but it is how I connect with you. If you consistently shut me down, I do take it personally, so make sure to communicate with me. Most importantly ... act like I'm the best lover ever!

Most items on each list can be applied to the opposite sex. It's a matter of remembering to pay attention and really caring openly, about the other.

CHAPTER 8

REIGNITING THE PASSION

"The value of the personal relationship to all
things is that it creates intimacy ... and intimacy
creates understanding ... and understanding
creates love."

—Anais Nin

Susan Bratton is a champion and advocate for every man
and woman who dreams of a passionate relationship.

Susan has authored 20 books and programs including
*Relationship Magic, The Passion Patch, 30 Romance Tricks
That Work Like Magic,* and *Revive Her Drive.*

She has a whole-hearted commitment to shame-free and
frequent sexual pleasure she believes is every man and
woman's birthright: *"After 21 years of marriage, I know from
experience that deep, passionate intimacy with my partner is
priceless: a priority that tops my list of must-haves alongside
good health and the love of family and friends. I have made it*

my mission to aid anyone who wants the kind of lovemaking that improves with age."

Susan is Chair Emeritus of the ad:tech conference and sits on the Board of Directors of ZEDO, Inc. She's a Silicon Valley Woman of Influence, a DEMO God and has been featured in The New York Times and on CNBC as well as appearing on ABC, CBS and NBC as the "Marriage Magician." She lives on beautiful Mt. Tamalpais in Marin, California with her husband and their teenage daughter.

Re-Sparking the Connection

Spoken from Susan.

A lot of people believe it's just the way it is, that your sex life, your intimacy, your connection and your zest for each other has to slowly erode. In fact, I'm here to tell you that it's just the opposite. Your connection with your partner can keep getting more rewarding and better if you know a couple simple things. It literally is an attitude, a mindset, and a belief. It takes communication skills and understanding. I'm going to share what I tell couples who want to get that passion back who have had success and have done so following these simple steps.

Your relationship can actually become more exceptional than when you were newlyweds. When you're newlyweds you don't know each other yet. You've got that new relationship energy but that does wear off. It's the oxytocin and dopamine, the feel good chemicals, running through your body. It is possible to get those elements pumping again. The fact that you've been together and you've been through things as a couple can actually make your relationship even better than when you first got together.

So what happens to the passion we felt in the beginning? Life gets in the way. Many things can contribute to the fact that we don't take time to romance each other. Difficulties with work, paying the bills, or even just having kids and having to put your attention on raising your children. Health issues can be a huge factor, as well. Whether it's physical or emotional, they're all the same. If you're depressed, it's no different than having cancer. You've got to deal with it.

Desire is your life force. It's your vitality. It's your zest. It's your lust. Those are just different words for the same thing. What happens when you're in pain is that pain covers desire. It pushes it down. When your libido drops, it comes from rustiness or lack of use. Lack of use comes from the other things that are contributing to taking your mind away from putting your attention on each other. It's important to learn how to co-regulate, how to soothe, and how to make each other feel loved, in order to maintain and grow your relationship vitality.

When the relationship vitality is absent couples begin living in a parallel universe. You're doing "parallel play" like 2-year-olds instead of playing together like older children do when they become aware of each other. It's about bringing your lives back together so whatever's gotten in the way, you are able to overcome those issues. Otherwise you end up in a platonic, rather than intimate relationship. A mutually supportive couple learns to cope with the cycles and rhythms of life, rather than skirting them. No matter how great my life looks or your life looks, we've all had our trials. We'll have some more. We all go through it. It's the human condition.

How to Regain the Passion and Intimacy

The one thing that determines long-term success in relationships is the belief that it's a journey, not a destination—you just keep on going. Julie Andrews recently lost her husband of 42 years, Blake Edwards. She said, "We took it a day at a time. That's how we stayed together." I believe what Andrews meant by this statement, is that they avoided getting too overwhelmed in life. They dealt with life's obstacles by maintaining perspective.

I'm going to introduce you to the Four Elements of Revival. Once you understand these you'll be able to take the necessary steps to rekindle passion. I believe probably 90% of marriages could be saved if couples understood the Four Elements.

I have talked to countless experts. I have compared hundreds of books about passionate relationships. I've studied the work of psychologists and psychiatrists. I've talked to experts and gurus. When I listen to them, they all say the same thing in different ways, that there are really four things to create long-term intimacy. I call them the Four Elements of Revival. I could have called them, "the four keys to re-sparking your relationship," or, "the four things you've got to do to get hot sex going again in your marriage." But because these are fundamental tenets for reviving the passion in your relationship, I chose to call them, The Four Elements of Revival. Now let me give you the list, then I will unpack what they are and how you revive your relationship.

The Four Elements of Revival

#1 Overcoming Resistance Issues

#2 Polarity

#3 Seduction

#4 Advanced Sexual Mastery

Overcoming Resistance

We start with overcoming resistance issues. The first thing to understand is if you're not feeling the passion, what is it that's preventing you? Is it that she's a workaholic or he's a workaholic or that the kids require attention.

I was just talking to my niece. She and her husband are working on possibly having him do a job change. They have two kids. They love their kids but feel they can never get away. They crept downstairs to their basement, to have a private conversation they didn't want their kids to hear. They don't want them to worry about moving or other issues, if he gets a different job. They had just gotten downstairs and the basement door opens. "Mommy, can I come down and play with my Legos with you guys?" I think we can all relate with this lack of privacy issue. Right?

What's the resistance to having sex? Are you exhausted? Do you not feel well? Are your kids constantly underfoot? Are you working so much you don't have any bandwidth left? Do you have health issues? What is it? For some couples it's, "My wife gained 200 pounds since we got married," or, "My husband has been in severe depression for years. I want him to make love to me. He can't get an erection." You have to deal with what it is. You have to look at your life and say, "Hey, if we're going to do this, we have to fix some of those problems or remove those obstacles."

Here's a big one... sexual shame, religious shame, growing up in a family where there was no touch. You never talked about sex, literally ignorance, lack of education such as, "I was a virgin when I got married. I've only done missionary position. I can't imagine doing more. I don't like to take off my nightgown. Please leave the lights off." This is the reality for many, many couples. There's absolutely nothing wrong with that happening. This is the situation you are in. How do we get you to love your body? How do we get you to manage your work so you can carve out some time? How do we get a sitter for the kids?

How do we get you to the point where we understand what's creating this depression so we can move through it together as a couple and get back on track, to overcome resistance? Always remembering that an emotionally well-connected couple learns how to do what is called 'co-regulation'. That means that you support each other in calming each other's nervous systems down because you can't really open yourself sexually to each other until you're able to just let go and relax.

Co-regulation is where you look in each other's eyes. You actually aren't busy doing other things. You look in your partner's eyes. You hug your partner. You hold each other. You cuddle. You spoon. You sit on your husband's lap. You hold each other on the sofa when you're watching a movie. That generates oxytocin and starts to increase that bond again. It's really about removing, fixing, compromising or going around the roadblocks between you and making love again.

How do you together support each other in removing the issue or minimizing it, to the point where you can move forward? That's how you overcome resistance. It takes some discussion, communication, compassion and empathy with your partner. Being mad at them because they won't have sex with you or they don't hug you enough isn't going to get you anywhere. You've got to get underneath what it is that's suppressing that desire. What's holding down your libido and keeping you from wanting your lover?

Polarity

The second element I call 'polarity' or the masculine/ feminine, the animal magnetism, that comes from the fact that men and women or the masculine/feminine are different and yet really evocative to each other, that magnetic pull of opposites.

We women these days, we have our own careers. We go off to work. We come home. We're living in a man's world in a lot of ways. We're very strong. We're very directed.

I was talking to my daughter. She has a new boyfriend. I was telling her about how to be feminine and what it is that men like about feminine women because she's a kick-ass, feminine girl. She said, "But Mom, how can you tell me I should be focused on being feminine when you're a feminist?" I responded by saying, "Because I'm a feminine feminist because I don't ever think that I can't play full-out. I can be as smart as I possibly can. I can be as accomplished as I possibly can. I can be as beautiful and healthy and loving and compassionate and kind and sexy. I can wear pink. I can enjoy every aspect of being an amazing, intelligent woman." Being strong or going out and being a warrior in your business doesn't preclude you from also walking around your house in flirty lingerie and some stripper shoes and seducing your husband. Why can't you have all that? You can. Those things aren't mutually exclusive.

They actually work beautifully together. Men love a strong, sexy woman who is not afraid to say that she is sexy. I think it's really important to understand that when you are trying to regain polarity in your relationship, when you're in the intimate times with your husband, you are not telling him what to do. You're inviting him to do things. It's just a slightly different mindset. It's putting on your naturally occurring feminine wiles. You're a seductress. You're an invitation to pleasure.

You're calling him out and bringing him to you and letting him know that he's desired and he's wanted. Why? Because for so many men, they're afraid to ask for sex once it's gone downhill because they sound needy, whiny, begging. The Number 1 question I get from women is, "How do I get my husband or my boyfriend or my partner to take control in the bedroom?" The Number 1 question that guys ask me is, "How do I get my partner to initiate sex with me?"

Everybody wants to have sex. Why is it that they're saying, "I'm waiting for him to get warm," or "I'm waiting for her to do it?" Your man needs to know you want him. She needs to know you want her. A woman at a primal level wants two things. *Listen up guys, two things.* She wants to know that you adore her. She wants to know what exactly you find sexually irresistible about her.

Try saying, "Baby, you're so adorable. I love you so much. You're such a good wife and such a good mother. You're such a darling woman. I just love to see how sweet you are to people." Then later you say, "Baby, your ass drives me crazy. When you walk through the living room and I see those buns a-shaking, I get a hard-on every time even after all these years. I look at other woman. They're pretty but I don't know what it is about you. You're the one. That body of yours, you're gorgeous. Your hair, I love the smell of you." That's what she wants to hear.

He wants to hear, "Baby, take me. I want you," so that he knows it's okay to proceed. Having that polarity, that masculine/feminine, where you sit on his lap, shake your booty for him, let him look at you naked, and/or put on lingerie or wear a sexy bra. It's when you call him from the office and say, "I'm wearing lacy panties. I'm going to let you look at them right now. I'm going to take a selfie. I'm going to text it to you because you're just a dirty little dog. I know you are." Everybody has his or her own personality. I'm just giving you some silly things to say that have huge impact.

Men's Role: The playfulness of that masculine/feminine dynamic is very, very important. Women love an erotic adventure. For men think of it that way. How do you lead her in the bedroom? A game plan helps. Tell her she's sexy. Have her sit in your lap. Giving her a foot rub is like magic in getting her relaxed and open. Tell her to let go and just surrender. Describe how you can see her getting turned on. Let her know you've got everything handled. The kids are gone. The room is warm. Her favorite sexy Barry White music is playing, or whatever you listen to that gets her turned on. Create a lover's space so all she has to do is show up and relax. Once she's ready, give her lots of orgasms. Read, study, and prepare for new ideas to help her reach orgasm. Your rewards will be great. Keep reading for tips on achieving this.

She'll respond by thinking, "Wow, he does know what he's doing! I want more."

Women's role: It's imperative that you give him feedback, so he understands what you like and don't. "Baby, I really like it when you pin my arms back on the bed like this, you get on top of me and you kiss me. I really like to be held down," or whatever your thing is. Tell him, "Here's a couple things that I would enjoy that you could spring on me during our love-making." He'll be thinking, "Thank God. She gave me some answers to the quiz. I'm going to do those," but then he'll just keep doing those 3 things. You've got to keep giving him some more. That's polarity. That's having fun, feeling playful, doing the masculine/feminine and teaching him what will turn you on so that he wins and when he wins, rewarding him.

"Oh my God, you did exactly what I wanted. I loved how you did it to me. That was awesome." Men love to serve the goddess. They love to give you exactly what you want but you have to tell them. Then when they do it, you must acknowledge them or they will feel taken advantage of, not respected, and not appreciated. Give your husband that appreciation and gratitude. That will start that fire going. You will be amazed.

Seduction

This is about understanding how to seduce a partner that you've been married to for 100 years. How do you keep it alive? How do you keep moving your partner toward more pleasure in order to seduce her?

Seduction starts with romance. Here is the way it works. Think about it as a stair stepping, or escalation. It's called erotic escalation. Men typically thought of it as foreplay. That's an old-timey word but nobody quite understood what it meant. Ideas like, "I think I'm supposed to do foreplay for 20 minutes but I don't actually know what that is. Is that oral sex?" That's actually sex. That's not foreplay.

Here's what women like. There are 5 different kinds of romance that get women at the same place as a man.

Number 1 is called *mindfulness*. You could call it presence. You could call it putting your attention on her. You could call it, "Put down your phone. Turn off your computer. Be with her. Have fun." Whatever that means for you, it's just being there with her and seeing life through her eyes. It's very, very important. It's dropping into being with your wife and really putting your attention on her. Go back to that playful, youthful time when you were completely in your bubble. She's going to want to have sex with you. You might not even have to do 2, 3, 4 and 5 but that's Number 1. Number 1 is slowing down and just being present with her.

Number 2 is the *sensate connection*; using your senses. Going back to the idea that you can calm each other's nervous systems down. You can hold her. You can give her hugs until she completely melts and relaxes in your arms. Men love to hold a woman. Women love to be held by a man. It's just a very primal thing. If you just take the time to do that, she'll start melting in your arms. She'll calm down. Her defenses will go down. She'll feel your attention. She'll begin to want you again. Gaze into her eyes. People are eye shy. If you're mad at your partner, you don't want to really look at them but once you start to look at them, they can't be mad at you for much longer because they begin to see past the anger.

The eyes are the windows to the soul. That's a soulful connection of lovemaking. That's how you get to the kind of lovemaking that's not just hot sex but it's intimate rapture where you're just playing off each other. You're feeling each other. You're just completely rebooted and refreshed because you've let the world go. You've fallen in with each other.

It's the sensation of stroking her skin that wakes up all these receptors. This is your sensual grid. Run your hands all the way up and down her body. Stroke her hair. Stroke her cheek. Kiss her eyelids. Kiss her neck. Touch her breasts but not her nipples. Don't go for Ground Zero until she's really reaching for you. Sensation is lovership.

Number 3 is *playful adventure*; thinking up fun things to do. The classics are the classics for a reason. Take her out on a walk in nature. Get outside together. Go for a walk.

Hold her hand. Stop and give her a hug. Give her a kiss. Look in her eyes. She'll be completely relaxed and ready to make love just after the walk. It's the idea of moving her body. When you're teaching a horse something, you walk the horse around in a circle.

You know how you train a horse? You move the horse's feet. Then he pays attention to you. It's how do you get someone to pay attention to you. Move them. How does the art of persuasion move them? You're moving their emotions. It's about creating movement. When you're moved by a movie, it sticks with you. Everything comes down to being able to move your partner. You want to create playful adventures that move her.

My husband and I just went to the wine country in our new convertible. We were on this lonesome road that was absolutely gorgeous. We had the top down. I told him to, "Push it. Push it. Go! Woo hoo." What was he doing? Why was that so romantic? He was moving me. All he was doing was driving a car but it was great. We had such a romantic evening that night. It was one of those days to remember because he moved me with playfulness and spontaneity.

Number 4, *erotic communication*. Women need to be adored. They want to feel sexually irresistible. This is an all-day-long kind of a thing. Text her. Send her an email. Take a picture. Write her a poem. Sing her a love song. Make her a playlist. Talk sexy to her. Talk dirty to her. Just keep it going, guys. I know that you guys are men of few words. I totally understand that, but we need you to say them because we really need to hear that we're awesome and that you love the stuffing out of us. It's incredibly important.

Number 5, *declarations*. These can be symbols, rituals, or traditions that express your love. Bring her flowers, write a poem, or deliver her favorite lunch. Do anything that's a visual, written, or tangible proof of your love.

Here's an example of a ritual that my husband does for me. He takes me shopping. I could perfectly well go to Nordstrom's myself, slap down my credit card and buy my thing that I need. Sometimes my husband will drive me to the mall, take me to Nordstrom and sit in the fitting room with me, as I try stuff on. He tells me what he likes. He pays for it. We have a joint account. It's not like he's actually buying it for me. But what I adore is when he handles everything and pays attention to me. The simple act of carrying the shopping bag makes me feel protected and cared for. After our shopping trip, he usually takes me out to lunch. We have a beer. Then he drives me home.

Oh my God, do I love that. I just love it when my husband takes me shopping. He buys me something. Then later when someone says, "That's such a pretty outfit," I respond, "Thank you. My husband bought it for me." See how that's the masculine/feminine you're taking care of.

That's super sweet for us. Many men think, "Really? That's what you want me to do? You don't want to just go to the mall and buy it yourself or get that thing on the Internet? Doesn't Amazon Prime deliver that?" It's so much more fun when you take us.

He wants you to feel sexy. He wants you to do anything and everything that it takes for you to feel like the goddess that you are so that when he makes love to you, you're not dis-empowering yourself by talking about your cellulite or you don't like your boobs or any insecurity. He loves the way you the look. You must let all that go. You're married to him. He loves you. He picked you. Enjoy.

Seduction Trilogy—Sexual Menus

Now you move into the seduction piece. We have a lot of seduction techniques that we teach at Personal Life Media. The one that I think is the most important comes from a program called the 'Seduction Trilogy'. Dr. Patti Taylor wrote it for me because I think she's the foremost in understanding how people who have been married forever can still bring each other more pleasure.

Women want to have lots of choice. Three choices are plenty for men. Women, we could probably handle more choices but when your guy says to you, "Would you like a foot rub, or would you like me to draw you a bath, or would you like to sit down on the couch and tell me about your day?" you're like, "Let's see. Could I have them all? Here's the order." Whereas, if your man asks, "Hey, do you want to have sex? Do you want to have a sex night?" Women will respond in this manner, "I absolutely do not want to have sex. Haven't even been thinking about it. Don't care to do it. It's a no!" Why? Because he started out with an offer that was too "big" for me.

This is why guys get the no's they get because they start with the big offer instead of the small offer. You start with small offers. You give your woman a menu of them. You can do this with men as well. "Would you like me to put on a negligee; would you like a back rub; or would

77

you like to go in the hot tub and drink a beer?" He's going to say, "I like them all and in this order." It's good to start out very small with women because we take a while to get turned on.

Giving her menus, running her menus and teaching your guy what kind of menus you like is also helpful but it's best if he just really pays attention to where you are, being vigilant about what's happening in your world. He's mindful. He needs to notice things such as, "She looks stressed out. Maybe I'll offer a neck rub, a foot rub, or a glass of white wine." Once again you'll probably respond with, "I'll take all three." That's the beauty of small offers. They're really easy to say yes to.

Then she starts saying yes to you instead of no. You can escalate from there and make it a slightly sexier offer and a slightly sexier offer. That is seduction - the kind of seduction that works.

Advanced Sexual Mastery Skills

The first thing I would say to women is 'orgasmic cross-training'. This is a term coined by sex coach, Sherri Winston. What it means is you probably have a path to achieve orgasm that is set. Usually it's the same path every time. How orgasmic cross-training works is you follow that same path and mix in a new way. Here's an example, if you use a vibrator to achieve orgasm, you would cross-train by using the vibrator and having intercourse at the same time. Over time, your body becomes trained to achieve orgasm during penetration without the vibrator. This practice can take your experience to a much more exciting level. Having intercourse with your husband now becomes more enjoyable and fulfilling.

The next advanced skill is understanding engorgement. Women have erectile tissue that has to be gotten erect to achieve orgasm. Guys tend to rush it. They tend to go in too early. She's not going to have an orgasm because she's not fully engorged. She's not ready. They think about it as "wet." (Frankly, so do a lot of women who are unaware of their need to be fully engorged before getting it on.) Guys think if she's wet she's ready when in fact those things are only partially connected. That's not the signal that she's actually ready to have an orgasm from intercourse.

If you want to have really great sex for the rest of your life with your partner, giving her lots of orgasms, in lots of ways, is the way to go. But she as the woman has to be willing to try to have them. She has to be willing to start as a beginner, to allow you to stumble a little bit; to try different techniques; to tell you what's turning her on and what's turning her off. She needs to communicate what's bringing her arousal up and what's suppressing her arousal. She has to know that you have enough moves and techniques that you're going to be able to go, "That didn't work. Let's try this one," like you've got this Swiss army knife of orgasm skills.

That comes from being prepared. That comes from knowledge, understanding women's anatomy, educating yourself, and getting online home study courses, like we offer at Personal Life Media. It's learning the communication skills along with the advanced sexual mastery techniques that allow a woman to express her full sexual potential. That's where we come in. We teach men and women all the things you can't find in the media and they sure don't teach you in school!

She's going to want more and more sex the more and more pleasure you give her. It's getting her to feel comfortable enough and to feel she trusts you enough to communicate her pleasure or what she wants to change. You can't let your ego get in the way. If you follow the tips I've shared, you will not only re-electrify your connection but also create a relationship that reaches the highest levels of passion and rapture where two become ONE.

CHAPTER 9

FINANCIAL FREEDOM

> "My problem lies in reconciling my gross habits with my net income."
>
> — Errol Flynn

Ever want to take duct tape and fully cover your partner's mouth, hands, and feet, not for intimacy play, but to get him/her to stop making financial decisions or spending in a manner not fitting your beliefs? No surprise that money is the number one reason reported for divorce. According to Farnoosh Torabi, celebrity financial advisor, financial opposites attract.

It doesn't matter if you have an abundance of money or live check-to-check. If one partner feels they are 'in the dark' or have little or no say in how the money is handled, it often leads to control issues.

If there are financial problems you've been afraid to reveal, use this time to come clean. Together you can develop a plan to overcome this *temporary* obstacle.

Remember, you're a team and when you both come from a place of love, problems get resolved far easier. The energy and stress put into hiding important issues, such as money, takes a huge toll on a relationship. Release the issue, deal with it, and move forward.

Mindset

When approaching your financial situation, think of it as a professional business meeting:

- Stick to the facts.

- Come up with reasonable solutions.

- Check your personal feelings, to make sure you're not allowing your emotions to interfere with making sound decisions.

Be a Big-Picture Thinker

When you approach your financial goals from a higher view—looking at the full picture of what you ultimately want—the shorter-term obstacles become less of a mental problem. Create the blueprint of how you are going to get to where you want and stay focused on that.

The fact that you have $30,000 in credit card debt simply becomes something that needs a solution. It's pointless to dwell on how you got there, *unless* the poor spending habits haven't changed. Instead, focus on what needs to be done to decrease debt and the steps you will take to get there.

I've compiled several tips adapted from financial experts including Farnoosh Torabi's, Dave Ramsey, best-selling author of several books on money, Michael E. Gerber, E-Myth founder, and my own personal studying of countless books and speaking with other experts. These tips and exercises will lead to a more harmonious fiscal situation, relieve strain, and help you achieve the lifestyle you both want.

How to Get Financial Control

- **Set Financial Goals:** Create both short and long-term goals. An example of short-term may be the purchase of a car, or planning a vacation. Long-term financial plans may include college, care for aging parents, life insurance, and retirement. Having the same financial goals will help diffuse complications, build trust, and magnify excitement toward your future. It will also give both of you a stronger sense of fiscal control.

Tools to Communicate

- **Schedule a Meeting:** Consider an ideal time that works for both of you. Make sure it's a time when you can fully focus in a relaxed manner.

- **Environment:** Think about going for a walk, out to coffee, working from your office, or staying at home with soothing music and a glass of wine. Will these things be the most effective and comfortable place for your conversation? It will depend on what needs to be accomplished. If your main intention is brainstorming, then a walk may be perfect. Obviously, if you need to write something, a walk won't work.

- **Preparation:** Meet at least one time per month for short-term goals. For longer-term goals, Torabi suggests one time per quarter. Set an agenda or topic (i.e. car, vacation, retirement) and do research prior to the meeting. Review accounts, read articles, and/or watch a finance webinar.

- **Make the Time:** Keep meeting time to 30 to 45 minutes. If it's typical that these meetings create a lot of stress, try having something positive planned after the meeting. Go to a movie, dancing, work out, or get together with friends. Basically, a date that takes both of you away from discussing money and puts your minds on something more pleasurable ... sex is also a good distraction (this is my tip)! If you were unable to resolve or cover all that was intended, make a follow-up meeting.

- **Brainstorm:** Discuss potential areas to save, decrease interest payments, items to cut out, insurance issues, etc. Can you get a reduction in property tax? Does it make financial sense to refinance the home? How much do you want to put away or invest?

- **Action Plan:** This is the most thrilling part - other than planning a vacation or a great new vehicle purchase. This is where you decide what needs to be completed before the next meeting; who is responsible for each task and how you will implement the action plan. The excitement comes from knowing you're taking steps to construct the life you two envisioned. Be sure to set a date for your next financial meeting.

Other Money Tips and Suggestions

- **Certified Financial Advisor:** An advisor can educate you on things you may not be aware of and be instrumental in helping you devise a plan based on your goals

- **Have 3 Accounts:** Set up three accounts - Yours, Mine, and Ours. This creates autonomy, gives independence, and helps avoid arguments.

- **Loss of Job:** When one partner becomes non-voluntarily unemployed that is when you need to work together the most! Supporting each other through the tough times is what builds the magic between two people. Those in a supportive partnership rebound much quicker, studies show. Take this opportunity to strengthen your relationship by building trust, love, and acting as a pillar to one another.

  Brainstorm and devise an action plan to move forward. Half the battle in life is confidence, which commonly suffers after job loss. Work to increase this, as opposed to tearing at one another. Remember to be a *Big Picture* thinker. There *will* be another job and all *will* be okay.

- **Lesser Income Earner:** Experts suggest attaching his/her income to a vacation, car, college, etc. to demonstrate the importance of their contribution.

- **Transparency:** Try not to cheat—romantically or financially! Torabi discussed the importance of sharing passwords and sticking with your plan. If you do stray, make sure you disclose this to your partner. This will help avoid confusion and other problems.

  NOTE: Mint.com is a fantastic FREE resource to help you manage your accounts.

CHAPTER 10

MAINTAINING YOUR NEW LIFESTYLE

"The sweaty players in the game of life always have more fun than the supercilious spectators."

—William Feather

Congratulations! If you've read the book in it's entirety, and completed the assignments, I bet you've noticed a shift in your mindset. You should also be seeing that positive things are happening in your life and in your relationship. I suggest re-taking the Live Sexy Relationship Assessment and compare your scores, from the quiz you took originally to your score now.

Here's the link: LiveSexyQuiz.com

You've begun the path to achieving your dreams together, but we need to keep the momentum going.

90-Day Goals

Remember to break down your large goals into 90-day increments. Focus on what needs to be done weekly, as well as daily, to keep it fresh and make the progress necessary.

The Z'Luxe Life 90 Day Action Planner is a fantastic tool to accomplish this. It keeps you organized, motivated, and is easy to use. You can check it out here: http://www.zluxelife.com/programs/

On-Going Assignments

Get a calendar and set dates for the following:

- Date Nights 1-2 times per month

- Mini Vacations—at least 2 per year

- Revisit Your Dream Life Goals—every 90 days

- Financial Meetings:

  ◊ Short-Term Goals: 1 time per month

  ◊ Long-Term Goals: 1 time per quarter

- *Celebrate and savor your relationship every day!*

What to do When There is Setbacks

An easy way to ensure you are staying on the right path is to mentally check your relationship POP. Remember Passion, Outlook, Play.

- *Passion*: What level is your relationship passion at? Are you paying attention to the romance, love, and intimacy?

- *Outlook*: Are you both focused on your goals and dreams, or have they been side railed?

- *Play:* Are you having fun together? How many times a day do you laugh?

If any of the above three elements are missing or not where you'd like them to be, it's a good indicator that they need attention. Life is continually evolving, thus you need to adjust too. Illness, time commitments, job changes, unplanned expenses, etc. can all easily distract us.

You may simply need to plan a date night to re-ignite the passion or schedule a financial meeting to adjust expenses or it may go much deeper, such as depression.

Whatever the issue is, listen, pay attention, and find a way to deal with it. It may require professional intervention. I always suggest keeping an open line of communication, to maintain the feeling of togetherness. Knowing you're in this life as a team makes conquering anything much less overwhelming.

Maintain your Positive Affirmations

If you slip into negativity, revisit your positive affirmations. Remind yourself of what you're grateful for in your partner, and in your life.

Be a Big Picture Thinker

What this means is to put things into perspective based on their overall importance and effect on your life. I watched one of my closest friends die from brain cancer. She had it for eight years before it took her life. She taught me a great life perspective. It was basically this: if something wasn't going to profoundly affect the future, don't waste much time worrying about it. Another way to look at it: focus on what *will* greatly influence the future.

Richard Carlson, Ph.D., wrote the series, *Don't Sweat the Small Stuff,* serving as a reminder that we need to stop stressing over inconsequential things and put our energy into that which truly matters.

A spouse that continually forgets to pick up his/her towel after showering will *not* profoundly affect your future, unless you choose to allow it to. Your child getting a poor grade on a test will not profoundly affect his/her future BUT helping to make it a learning experience, to aid in improving their academic skills, will. Make sense?

Big Picture Ideas

Your relationships, your dreams and goals, your health are all examples of big picture ideas. Spending time nurturing, planning, and implementing steps to grow or improve each of these areas will always be of immense value, now and in the future.

I would love to hear about the positive changes you've made and the improvements it's led to in your life and relationship.

Here's to living your Z'Luxe Life!

ABOUT MIDORI VERITY—
IT STARTED WITH A
MIDLIFE CRISIS!

Have you had that moment where you felt your life was a huge disappointment? Have you ever been stuck on the hamster wheel of life? I have. On May 11—it was my 40th birthday—I woke up with an overwhelming, soul-filling, sense of failure and sadness. I realized immediately why I felt the way I did. My life was half over (at least that was my thought), and I had not achieved the dreams I had set in my youth. I wanted to be a CEO of a Fortune 500, have a ginormous home, be respected by the world, and feel unstoppable. I was 40 and felt as though I had no control over the direction of my life. Staying on the current path was definitely NOT what I wanted.

I knew I should be happy with my two wonderful boys, my loving husband, and the decent life we lived. My husband and I ran our own business, for around 15 years, that was relatively successful. However, I *hated* it with all my heart, from the tip of my toes to the end of my longest hair on my head. I felt complete burnout, but didn't know how to get out. The thought of having to continue with it for another 20 years was astronomically repulsive, making me want to physically hurl every time I thought of that horrendous possibility. We had gotten used to our lifestyle. There was no way to go back to working for someone, and the fear of not being able to provide the life our kids deserved, was paralyzing. I knew it was up to me to find another income source but what?

What did I really want? I no longer had the desire to be part of a Fortune 500. I enjoyed being self-employed, just not the company I currently owned. I wanted a company that I was excited about, was unique to me, and was helpful to others. My husband and I came up with a few business ideas but none panned out for one reason or another.

My business continued to control me and I began associating my husband with it. I had finally gotten to the point where I just wanted out. Did I want out of just the business or was it from my marriage too? He refused to sell until we had another viable business or income stream - he's so damn practical! I was done being practical and was willing to live in a tent if necessary ... ok, just kidding. I do require a *bit* of luxury. Based on this reality, I began to blame my husband for our situation and the self-inflicted entrapment. I loved him with all my heart but my depression and absolute compulsion for escape was beginning to take over.

My journey in search of a new direction began. I stopped watching TV, decreased my social life to almost nil (which is huge for me, I have a psychological need for fun, seriously ...), and spent that time devouring self-improvement books written by top psychologists in cognitive and behavioral therapy. I started going to seminars and watching every expert and guru available on YouTube. Neuroscience became an obsession. I even went to a hypnotherapist for the first time. I began to use what I was learning to change my mindset. I went from focusing on the negative to seeing and living the positive.

I was invited to a business seminar where I met a brain science expert. He intrigued me further about the power of the brain, and how we can use it to accomplish unbelievable heights, squashing out once perceived obstacles and challenges. I ordered his book as soon as I returned home. I used the suggestions he made to change my thought patterns and beliefs, many of which are in this book. I quickly realized the power of the brain and began studying *everything* I could about brain power, aka Neuroscience, to help people on their path to greatness or whatever one wants. It was clear, I was on to something life changing.

Throughout this turmoil and other challenging times in our lives, my husband and I have been able to come out stronger emotionally and physically, as a couple. I will admit, there have been times when something took over my mind, and words I shouldn't say did come out. Luckily, I have learned more control and calmness since then. My husband has expressed many times how he recognizes and appreciates this change! Despite my occasional regression, we were always the couple others looked to when they were experiencing challenges. My advice consistently worked, and it was based solely on what my husband and I did to keep things going in our marriage.

Everything began to click then. It became clear to me that I had a gift to share. I wanted to help couples achieve a happier life together. I paired my desire to help others with the vast amount of knowledge and education I learned along my journey and now I lead couples to a better life.

Today, I am achieving unbelievable goals, things I would never have thought possible 5 years ago. I am living an incredibly fulfilling and exciting life, and I'm happy to share it with you; plus save you time. I hope you found the solutions needed to start you on a positive path with your partner. Remember, a relationship is not a straight line but a curvy one. Expect the rough spots and take comfort in knowing you're in this together. Two is better than one!

I invite you to learn more about my *Live Sexy Relationship System*, to go deeper into creating the life you and your partner have always wanted. I'd love to have you a part of our wonderfully positive, exciting, and supportive community.

Web site: http://www.zluxelife.com/programs/

www.ingramcontent.com/pod-product-compliance
Lightning Source LLC
LaVergne TN
LVHW051810080426
835513LV00017B/1892